BLOCKCHAIN REVOLUTION:

The Era of Bitcoin, Ethereum, and other Cryptocurrencies

By: Rick Maverick

BLOCKCHAIN REVOLUTION:

Copyright © 2018 by Rick Maverick.

Table of Contents

Introduction

• About the book

This book is a one-stop attempt at bringing the Blockchain technology to the masses by a clear and precise look at the different technologies and concepts that helped bring the technology into scalable dimensions.

Never has there been a more disruptive invention in how money is created, distributed and liberalized by ensuring that the power of deciding what to do with one's wealth lies with that person.

Starting as a simple way of transferring cash, cryptocurrencies have spawned different ideas that were hitherto not possible. It is now possible to carry out crowdfunding to sponsor wonderful ideas through crowd sales of cryptocurrencies, which removes the decision of which businesses will scale from banks' boardrooms to the street.

And this is instructive in a world that knows no restrictions to the way it thinks about business and the creation of money anymore.

Cryptocurrencies are even starting to question the centralized decision making when it comes to societal priorities. It is now possible to list 'common good' projects on a Blockchain and hardcode how to distribute a particular percentage of mining rewards.

If you have never understood anything about bitcoin and the other cryptocurrencies, then this is a great place to start.

What you will take away from reading this book

- A good capability of identifying and understanding Blockchain technologies.
- Understand how a Blockchain works.
- Understand how decentralization is a-chieved through consensus algorithms.
- Understand how to invest in cryptocur-rencies.
- Find resources that you can find online and continue understanding the technol-ogy better.
- Find out the relationship between de-centralization and current government regulation
- Have a good grasp of what the future holds for cryptocurrencies

1. Blockchain Technology; a New Paradigm

1.1. What is a Blockchain?

When computers (or nodes) are dedicated to a global network where they can be used to store a regularly updated database of transactions or records that are shared and immutable, they are said to be operating in a Blockchain.

Each of these computers is obligated to do the work of verifying the transactions, adding them to the ledger and broadcasting this fact to its 'peers.' This broadcasting ensures that all the other computers update the information of that transacttion to have the same information across the board.

To incentivize them, a reward system is incorporated into the ledger coding so that if a computer can prove it did these tasks successfully, then it is rewarded in a way that all the other computers understand. This reward is usually done using an inbuilt token, or a coin, which is transferable from each member of the community to another.

No computer is superior to the rest when it comes to administrative power, and the Blockchain is run by consensus. The Blockchain is the first truly decentralized and highly effective human system.

1.2. How Does a Blockchain Work?

Whenever a transaction is done, the sender attaches a small fee that works as 'gas' for driving the transaction into the network. The transaction enters into a pool where it must be picked by one of the nodes, announced to the network, and once the network agrees that the transaction is valid, the node then embeds it into a block and claims the fee.

For a node to be able to create and fill a block, it must earn the right to be allowed to be the one doing that at any particular time. This is because there are so many nodes trying to earn the reward and the fees. So each Blockchain tries to create a way that ensures that nodes compete in a 'race' and can prove that they have won this right.

2. The Mix That Makes the Blockchain

It is through the use of several technologies that already existed that **Satoshi Nakamoto** was capable of making the Blockchain technology possible. Here we look at a summary of these technologies that used together solved the problem of 'double spending' and created bitcoin and other cryptocurrencies.

2.1. Cryptography

Cryptography is the process of turning ordinary plain text into coded text and vice-versa. Once encrypted, it can be transmitted in a particular form that can only be decrypted by those who are intended to receive the information.

When data encrypted, is protected from theft or alteration, and can also be used for authentication of the transaction.

Though flaws in the algorithms that are used to encrypt data can be found, with time security can be achieved with a higher degree of confidence than in other conventional data storage and transmission technologies.

2.2. Decentralization

One of the real inventions of the bitcoin protocol was decentralization. When Satoshi created the algorithm that was to run the Blockchain, he also created a system that could not be controlled from a central source. He envisioned a system that would be able to be managed by a set of hardcoded rules enforceable by everyone, every time.

This was done to ensure that malicious attacks cannot be executed on a central point of failure and that the system would have many other players to reject the attacked nodes.

2.3. The Distributed Ledger

The only way that decentralization would work perfectly is if any of the computers, or nodes as they are called, would have all the information that any other computer has about the transactions and any messages that have been transmitted by any member of the network. This is what is called a Blockchain, or simply a ledger.

Every time a number transaction is added to the ledger, the computer that does that immediately distributes the newest version of the ledger to all the other nodes so that they can store the current state.

2.4. Management through consensus

The Blockchain technology can only be as successful as its member place importance on the consensus algorithm that runs each Blockchain.

It is therefore very important for the early developers of a Blockchain to conceive the consensus mechanism comprehensively ahead of adoption so that the Blockchain can have a chance of survival.

If the idea behind the Blockchain is not well thought out, either the Blockchain will not be joined by anyone, or it will collapse through disagreements and hard forks.

2.5. The Block

A block is just a 'container' which stores transactions and must have an identity that ties in with the most recent block, forming a Blockchain. Each Blockchain identifies how it wants the nodes to create the blocks. If the Blockchain also needs the creation of its token to be evenly distributed, it includes the minting of a new number of the token as a reward to the node that 'discovers' a valid block. This is called mining.

2.6.   Mining and Proof of Work

How are blocks 'created'?

Any node on the bitcoin network can create a block.

When this happens, several things are needed;

- The hash of the previous block.
- The cryptographic identities of all the transactions that are to enter the new block.

A nonce, which is a random number created by the Blockchain to create the randomness of the calculation.

There are many of nodes trying to find a valid bitcoin block every 10 minutes. Only one block can be mined and added to the Blockchain. Mining is, therefore, a race against time. The Blockchain has to find a way for only one node to win the race every 10 minutes.

The Parameters that enable even bitcoin mining.

It is estimated that bitcoin mining will come to an end around the year 2140.

When writing this, there are already 16.8 million bitcoins in circulation. This leaves 4.2 million bitcoins to be mined.

So the question is, how will they be mined evenly in 123 years?

The code that runs bitcoin cuts the block mining reward by half every 210,000 blocks, which is roughly four years.

Only around 2160 blocks can be mined every two weeks. This is because it is only possible to mine one block every 10 minutes.

The code adjusts the rate by increasing or decreasing the difficulty of solving the hash rate that is used to earn the right to mine a block.

The rewards started at 50 BTC from the genesis block, and this has been halved twice since 2009 to the current reward of 12.5 BTC.

Why Proof of Work (PoW)?

Since every mining node is 'creating' a block, there has to be a way of ensuring that, of thousands of blocks being created at the same time, only an average of 1 bitcoin block is successfully solved in 10 minutes.

Nakamoto found a way of accomplishing this using 'Proof of Work.'

When a computer creates a hash for a new block, it computes a cryptographic equation using three variables, namely the identity of the previous block, the identities of all the prospective confirmed transactions and a random number known as a nonce.

The hash thus created is of a definite length and must be compared to the current value availed by the Blockchain. This value is availed every two weeks or roughly 2160 blocks. The valid values must be lower than or equal to the availed value.

If the value is not valid, the node will pick another nonce and recompute. All mining nodes will continue this random process until a valid block identity is found. The race is won, and the mining of the next block begins.

The computation of new blocks is very random, and billions of guesses are done by many computers, at the expense of electricity and computational power.

Once a computer wins, it then updates the distributed ledger and broadcasts the current state to all the other nodes. That block is said to be mined.

The node is now set to claim a reward of newly minted bitcoins.

So, how are the fees and rewards claimed?

Confirmation of a block happens whenever a child block is hashed and added to the block in question. This is done by validating nodes in the network. The transaction then left in a memory pool awaiting confirmation.

There are transaction fees attached to each transaction to incentivize miners, they will only pick your transaction when hashing a new block if it has attractive fees.

If a miner creates a block that has your transaction, they will claim the fees attached to the transaction.

The block will now await confirmations, which are additions of child blocks, in the Blockchain. These confirmations happen whenever a subsequent block is added to the one which contains your transaction.

The bitcoin core only allows a block that has 100 child block confirmations to deposit the reward to the block miner's wallet.

What happens to discarded blocks?

For one block to claim a mining reward every 10 minutes, many are simply discarded, and the transactions that have not been included in the mined block are returned to the mem pool to be mined again.

This is the wastefulness of the Proof of Work algorithm that was intended to accord bitcoin real-world value as it could be quantified using the electricity that was expended to come up with the mined reward. Imagine how much electricity and computational power expended by thousands of computers every 10 minutes for one of them to claim the reward.

How does the Blockchain prevent the fraud?

The Blockchain technology pursues 'a single truth.' Miners will only add a valid block to the longest chain of blocks. An interesting scenario happens if two blocks are hashed and found to be valid at the same time interval, they are said to be 'forking.'

In the next block to be mined, when the miner chooses one of the two forking blocks randomly, the chances are that other miners will only add to the one with a child block to pursue the single truth and hasten the block reward process. The shorter arm of the fork will be abandoned, and the block or blocks thus formed will be said to have been orphaned.

The blocks in the shorter chain will still stay in the Blockchain, but the miner will not get any rewards.

The mining rules allow for claimed rewards to only mature after a block commands more than 100 consecutive child blocks.

That is when the mining reward appears in the wallet of the miner after being deposited by the protocol. By then, there cannot be two claimants of the same reward.

Aren't there many wasted efforts to mine?

Of course, there are millions of computations that go to waste when a mining round is in play. That is the point of mining. Computers that win the race have to prove to others that they found a valid block. Each computer can do the winning hash and compare the block identity to those that they know were valid identities at the time.

When they do this, they are using hindsight, and the verification is instant. This way, they can verify in a test without the need for trusting the winning node that actual work was done. This gives the winning node the opportunity to claim the reward for that particular block.

3. The Pain Points Being Addressed by the Blockchain

3.1. Means of Exchange

Most cryptocurrencies are also used as a means of exchange that has a value which is agreeable to the Blockchain. This makes it possible to trade with each other, instantly, cheaply, and conveniently. Thus, these currencies have the potential of replacing centralized money systems like US Dollars, The Euro, The GBP and any other legal tender.

3.2. E-Commerce

The current problem with online buying and selling is mostly centered on trust. You buy things online, and you have to trust that once the money leaves your hands, the item you get when it is delivered is what you saw online and decided to buy.

With smart contracts, the Blockchain can hold your money and await a signal from you that you have received what you wanted before it releases the money to the seller. And the seller will be able to see that you have released the money to the Blockchain so that they feel safe to release the item.

The smart contract can also be able to act in several ways based on your instructions, including splitting one payment to several vendors, and also instructing the delivery service where to deliver, etc.

3.3. Insurance

In a decentralized insurance environment, it is possible to make insurance cheaper by transparently agreeing to record the money that is being paid by contributors, and where it is going. This is because the Blockchain has no individual profiteer or power broker, and all contributions are publicly declared on the Blockchain.

3.4. Medical Records

Medical records can be the transaction of focus, enabling each person to have a permanent and worldwide available medical history that is verified and instantly availed to any practitioner wherever you go, so long as you give proper authorization.

With Digital money, it is now possible now to transfer money instantly, globally. A real estate Blockchain can allow its members to know where properties are cropping up, and queue up with ready funds to purchase a property they choose, wherever it is, at a price they can afford.

Smart contracts can also allow the deeds to change hands and the transaction to be permanently recorded into the Blockchain, proving who owns what in a way that cannot be corrupted by anyone, in any way.

3.5. Venture Capital

With decentralized systems, anyone can invest any amount of money into a company or an idea that operates on a Blockchain. All they will need is to purchase enough tokens of that venture to gain the percentage ownership they want to command.

Though that does not mean they own shares in the business, it means that they have a valuable asset that is in demand from those who don't have it and are willing to pay a premium to get it, especially if the token is the only way to do business in the Blockchain.

3.6. Decentralization of Currency

Through the use of the Blockchain technology, the currency has been decentralized. It is now possible for anyone to create a currency so long as they believe that they can form a vibrant community of people to use that currency.

As much as many legalities and cyber-attack challenges still exist with this technology, it is no longer a matter of if, but when, cryptocurrencies will become mainstream. Wealth creation, distribution and even decision making on what to use it for is now decentralized, and the Blockchain network does not restrict how this is done.

3.7. Anonymity and Security of Information

Unlike centralized systems where full identity disclosure is an essential part of engaging in financial matters, the only identity in bitcoin is the wallet public key, which is a pseudonymous string of characters that have nothing to do with someone's identity.

Though pseudonymous systems like bitcoin can be forced by authorities to give information that could lead to an identification of the entities behind the wallets, Blockchains are working towards ensuring that anonymity is bolstered using various technologies. When exploring the altcoins, it will be clear that some use anonymity as a selling point.

4. Important Dates in Bitcoin's Life

4.1. 2007 – Nakamoto Begins the Journey

On 31st October 2008, Satoshi Nakamoto, a cryptographer who has remained anonymous to date, released the Bitcoin white paper.

It detailed a stupendously simple method of combining several technologies that existed beforehand in creating a peer-to-peer online cash transfer system that depended on consensus for confirmation of transactions and not on trust.

He released Bitcoin Core, the protocol that he created, on 3rd January 2009. Bitcoin was the unit which would be used to transfer value peer to peer, and it became the first successful digital crypto-currency.

There were other previous attempts at creating digital cash, but they all went short of expectation especially when it came to eradication of the double spend problem

Decentralization was also not well understood until the bitcoin white paper was released, and this was so because most previous currencies had not created an autonomous open-source system, making it easy for regulators to quickly clamp down on the development.

Even though no one knows who Satoshi is, the first people to adopt the coin are well known.

Satoshi sent the first 10 Bitcoin (BTC) to Hal Finney, the cryptographer who developed the Re-usable Proof of Work algorithm.

However, the foremost personality in Bitcoin is Gavin Andresen. He took over the running of Bitcoin Foundation in 2010. Originally, only cryptographers experimented with bitcoin. They stayed and worked with the system until they were convinced that they could publicize it

Bitcoin's Value was originally set by negotiation between any two parties before a transaction.

The most famous transaction involving bitcoin was the 10000 bitcoins what Laszlo Hanyeks, a cryptographer himself who was experimenting with bitcoin, used to purchase two pizzas at Papa John's.

Going by the current bitcoin value, those bitcoins would now be worth $150 million!

4.2. 2009 – Bitcoin comes to life

On 3rd January 2009, Satoshi mined the Genesis Block. It had only one transaction, and a message in the transaction referred to the day's financial news. Satoshi intended to ensure that future members of the network were aware of everything he did and that he did not intentionally mine a lot of the bitcoins before releasing the Blockchain.

The Genesis Block is the first ever block created in the bitcoin Blockchain, and indeed in the whole cryptocurrency space. With it, a new way of minting money was created.

Bitcoin's original version (version 0.1) was released on 9th January 2009 at SourceForge. With the release, bitcoin stopped being just a whitepaper on some mailing list to the first ever Blockchain.

In mining the genesis block, and indeed for the next ten days, Satoshi mined all bitcoins entirely alone during the pilot phase, as he continued to convince other cryptographers to join the bitcoin network. At that time, at the time they used their CPUs for mining.

He continued to collaborate with other members of the bitcoin network in doing all modifications of the system until December 2010 when he gave control to Gavin Andresen. Andresen continues to run the network.

4.3. 2010 Bitcoin's First Hack, and GPU Mining

On 6th August 2010, the first major bitcoin protocol vulnerability was spotted. It allowed for transactions to be put on the Blockchain without proper verification, which allowed users to bypass bitcoin consensus and create many bitcoins.

On 15th August, this vulnerability was exploited to create 184 billion bitcoins. However, within hours, the fraudulent bitcoins were erased from the network, and the system was hard forked to create a more secure version. This remains the only major vulnerability of Bitcoin Core to date.

Meanwhile, as the technology started gaining traction and more and more people started mining bitcoin, the difficulty in mining started going up, and people started to find more efficient mining methods. Soon, video graphic processing units previously used for games were identified as better at mining than normal CPUs. This discovery is mainly credited to Artforz, a bitcointalk user.

4.4. 2011 – Dollar Parity, Bitcoin Magazine and The Genesis of Mining Pools

On 9th February 2009, Bitcoin reached dollar parity for the first time in its history.

In September 2011 **Vitalik Buterin**, together with **Mihai Alisie**, co-founded Bitcoin Magazine. It was the first magazine about cryptocurrencies. He continued working with the magazine until he left to start the **Ethereum Blockchain**. The Magazine is currently owned by BTC media. We will discuss more concerning the Ethereum in Chapter 6.

Mining pools also started coming into being around 2011. It had become apparent that GPU mining could be improved by pooling resources and increasing the chances of discovering blocks. By early 2011, Slush Pool, one of the earliest mining pools was fully operational.

There has been a lot of talk over how mining pools could attain centralization, especially after pools like Ghash.io and BTCguild came close to commanding more than 50% of bitcoin's mining power, a dangerous undertaking that could be used to shut down the network by attacking the pool.

However, other ways of controlling this are being devised, including decreasing the difficulty of mining to allow more people to join the mining network and therefore minimize the risk of centralization.

4.5. 2012 – Bitcoin Foundation, Halving, and Conferences

On 27th September, Bitcoin foundation was launched. Its main aim has been to oversee the development of the network.

Satoshi hardcoded the supply of bitcoin to 21 million and ensured that they would be mined over a long period. A block is created every 10 minutes, and Satoshi coded the Blockchain to originally reward each miner with 50 BTC per confirmed block. This reward would be halved every 210,000 blocks, and therefore the first halving happened on November 28, 2012.

It was feared that the halving event would destabilize the network with miners leaving the network, but it seems that this was not the case because anyone leaving would be quickly replaced with someone else who could mine the newly decreased difficulty and still accommodate the halved reward.

4.6. 2013 – Crime Busting, Space travel, and Education

It is not enough to talk about bitcoin mining without mentioning the beginning of usage of Application Specific Integrated Circuits, which is a fancy name for a computer that was designed to only do one thing. That is to mine bitcoin. ASICs simply put the small guys out of bitcoin mining and ushered in the mining pools and farms.

By now, miners started migrating their operations to China to take advantage of cheap electricity and cheaper hardware.

By 9th April, bitcoin's price hit $200, and financial and mainstream business institutions started taking note of the technology.

Virgin Galactic announced that they would start accepting bitcoin for space travel, and the University of Nicosia in Cyprus announced that they would receive payments in bitcoin for tuition.

Unfortunately, criminals encroached on the pseudo-anonymity of bitcoin to begin an all-around drug ring on Silk Road. It had gone on for some time, and on 2nd October, the FBI shut it down, causing a price drop in Bitcoin.

4.7. 2014 – The Mt. Gox Hack, Gaming, and the Hash Race

In February 2014, Mt. Gox, the biggest bitcoin exchange in the world, operating from Shibuya, Japan, closed all operations. They had just lost 850,000 bitcoins to a hack or roughly 7% of the volume traded there. They filed for protection against customer debt.

There was also a nominal drop of the bitcoin to the price of a penny which lasted minutes but which allowed for massive 'asks.'

Initial suspicions were that Mark Kapelês, the French proprietor of Mt. Gox, had embezzled the bitcoin.

After an arrest by the Japanese authorities in July 2015, some of the bitcoin mission was shown to have been disappearing from Gox's hot wallet since 2011. He pleaded not guilty, and probably rightly so, as most of the BTC has been found with a Russian money launderer known as Alexander Vinnik.

Alexander's connection to the lost coins has been established.

Bitcoin has threats from governments, financial institutions, hacks and outright thieves. However, all seem to bolster its standing as a current day currency. It seems that even negative interest in the currency seems to make more and more users learn and start using cryptocurrencies.

Because of the recovery of stolen bitcoin, the members of the bitcoin network seem to grow as the confidence of apprehension of malicious attackers of the network seems to grow by the day.

In fact, by early December, Microsoft started accepting bitcoin payments.

4.8. 2015 – Bitcoin Enters UK Banking

June 2015 saw the release of BitLicense in New York, which is the common name given to all virtual currency operating licenses.

By October, the European Union Court of Justice clarified that bitcoin and other cryptocurrencies were currencies, and not goods or services, and their trading could not be subjected to taxation.

Meanwhile, a lot of debates, meetings, legal processes conferences were happening in the UK to enable the inclusionary processes that would bring bitcoin to UK banking.

4.9. 2016 – Japan Legalization and Video Games

On 4th March 2016, The Japan Times reported that the Japanese Cabinet had approved some bills which would assist the banking sector to expand their flexibility when it came to Information Technology. This marriage of banking and IT is being referred to as 'FinTech' in emerging technical par-lance.

At the same time, the cabinet also took into stock the rising importance of cryptocurrencies and the new bills recognized them as a payment method.

Japan had just rendered legitimacy to currencies, something that many economies, including the US, were struggling with.

Another major boost in the popularity of bitcoin became the prevailing political upheavals in major economies of the world in the year.

When separatist politics of the Brexit combined with an unforeseen Trump Election in the US, and other political uncertainties in Europe, it was natural for people to look for a worldwide independent monetary pacifier that was not directly hinged on the political policies or decisions of one country, and bitcoin was always there to offer that shoulder.

Another emerging truth is that the Blockchain technology is a true innovation that could make operations even in traditional banks very secure and efficient. It would simply be ignorant for banks to ignore the digitization of financial assets with the logistical, security and cost savings that it would create for everyone.

If people are trading assets peer to peer, bank tellers will become moot. Expensive money dispensers like ATMs could be bypassed. Even interbank money exchanges could be done paperless, hassle-free. Banks have therefore appointed to learn the technology and how they can use it to harness its properties, and also to be able to survive when full adoption becomes a reality.

4.10. 2017 – The Bitcoin and Altcoin Explosion

Bitcoin had a humongous year in 2017. Opening the year at a then-record price of $1,000, it rose a whopping 1300%, against the predictions of most pundits, to close the year at around $14,500, after rallying to almost $20,000 in early December.

All this happened as the currency received massive body blows in the form of consensus splits, bad publicity, failed improvements and high price volatility.

In January, China rocked the bitcoin boat by announcing that it was investigating potential cases of fraud. From a high of $1,300, BTC crashed to almost $780.

By March, it had shaken off the aftershocks of the Chinese crackdown, only to hit another deadlock when the perennial Winklevoss brothers were denied by the Securities and Exchanges Commission of the US the chance to build a bitcoin linked exchange fund.

By April, Japan declared bitcoin a legal currency, and this marked the first major endorsement of the coin that ushered in a belligerent journey that ensured better times to come.

August 1 brought the big hard fork that created bitcoin cash (BCH) when a fall out about the size of the blocks started creating anxieties with the investors.

China banned all ICO activity on September 4, and bitcoin crashed again at a price of $3,226. The only other bad publicity issue was when Jamie Damon, the CEO of JPMorgan called bitcoin a fraud.

After that, bitcoin went on a bullish rise, hitting $7,500 by November 8th.

When CME Group and CBoe Global Markets requested for permission to trade in bitcoin futures, the Commodity Futures Trading Commission approved the trade and bitcoin hit five figures for the first time in history, reaching almost $20,000 before correcting to a stability of around $15,000.

5. The Rise of the Altcoins

5.1. Understanding Bitcoin's Pain Points

The anonymity question

In a conventional bank, your details such as your ID number, photograph, and even your driver's license or passport are the identities that allow you to access money. This information can be used to track your activities because all transactions under your account are logged in the bank's server.

So, if somebody is targeting your account, all they need to do is hack the bank, and all your information will be available to them. You could lose your money, get prying eyes into who you send money to and probably provide clues into other aspects of your life.

This is what regulators do. However, bitcoin's promise was a better level of anonymity where your details were not known to the network. However, they could only achieve pseudo-anonymity.

Bitcoin is mainly minted by miners, but most people who have bitcoin buy it from the miners using exchanges that have various levels of authentication, including a request for the same details banks use.

This could be used to unmask the identities behind the crypto wallets holding bitcoin.

If your transaction details could be anonymous, such problems would be easy to avoid. This is why anonymity is attractive to many users. It appears that bitcoin's original code did not accord the level of anonymity that was desired by many.

Mining Difficulty, PoW, Scalability and Transaction Fees

As we have seen earlier, the bitcoin network is maintained by miners, who have to use electricity and computation power to mine bitcoin. This process is wasteful and was designed to give bitcoin security, and many miners would be working to win the race to mine a block, thus securing the system from attacks.

However, because of the escalation of innovation into the mining rigs to increase processing speeds and therefore compete better at getting bitcoin rewards, the difficulty to mine has reached very high heights, in which only a few established miners can afford.

Meanwhile, bitcoin has been gaining popularity due to the advantages it presents with digital peer to peer transfer of money. Millions of users are now using bitcoin, and with this comes the issue of a massive number of transactions awaiting confirmation.

Since the protocol allows miners to choose and pick which transactions must enter into the Blockchain, and transactions are assigned a fee to incentivize the miners, only higher fees are attractive for miners to confirm blocks.

This then means that wait times for confirmation of some transactions keep going higher.

Another scalability problem has been the block size. A bitcoin block has for long stood at 1 MB, which was okay at inception but is no longer sustainable.

Because of their power, the miners have been voting down block size increments to rake in fee profits as users try to 'jump the queue,' and this has started to become a sticky point in the Blockchain.

Improvement Suggestions and Fallouts

So whenever there has been any suggestions for improvements in block sizes, conferences have been held, members have been lobbied and promises have been made to support the Blockchain improvements.

However, the road has not been easy, where sometimes some of the players, especially miners, have placed the profits before the common good of the Blockchain. This has had the effect of groups of members deciding to either execute improvements of the Blockchain protocol or simply leave the network.

5.2. Bitcoin Hard Forks, and the Genesis of Altcoins

With bitcoin being open source, with no patents and literary no regulation, it was just a matter of time before other developers started running their networks.

It is easier to understand forks by using the examples of what has happened in bitcoin.

Decentralization has brought transparency and the ability to manage through consensus rules to the internet of money. However, people join crypto networks with the understanding that the rules are to be followed in an exact fashion to maintain a current consensus.

If there are any changes to the rules that are accepted by the whole network, they are called a 'soft fork.' They do not result in a loss of compatibility with the earlier version of the protocol.

If the new rules end up altering the consensus so much so that it is not possible to have overall acceptability, this results in a 'hard fork,' in which some members continue with the old Blockchain, and others start mining the Blockchain with the improvements.

It is interesting to note that the majority will remain with the original name of the Blockchain, even if it is the new Blockchain that had implemented improvements, as happened with the Ethereum Blockchain when Ethereum Classic was created.

The Hard Fork is the burden of decentralization.

Apart from the bitcoin pains that we have seen before, let us summarize the reasons why Blockchains hard fork:

- Rising of transaction queues with an increase in the popularity of the Blockchain affecting processing speed, transaction fees and wait times.

- Malicious attacks on the Blockchain that target weaknesses in the cryptographic code. This could allow for theft of crypto, or sabotage of the network's operation.

- Pre-ordained improvements which are expected by the network and are a part of the development and fortification of a network.

- Future innovations that could render the current technology obsolete. For example, the Blockchain technology is still not ready for quantum computers and the power they might bring into the cryptographic space.

Bitcoin XT: The first fork – Dec 2014

In bitcoin lingo, a change in the consensus algorithm is executed using what is known as a Bitcoin Improvement Proposal (BIP).

Mike Hearn and Gavin Andreesen used BIP 101 to execute a bitcoin hard fork in December 2014. They planned to improve the block size of the blocks from

1 MB to 16 MB and in the process improve the confirmation speed to 24 transactions per second from the current seven.

At first, they recorded quite some success, with 2000 validating nodes by August 2015. Miners, however, have shied away from this fork due to lower fees. The support for this altcoin has been waning.

Bitcoin Unlimited – Jan 2016

Another interesting hard fork started in January 2016. Bitcoin unlimited (BTU) intended to have user-defined block sizes, with a higher limit of 16MB.

Exchange platforms and wallets would be allowed to set the block sizes they accept. Miners would, therefore, choose to work with the exchanges and wallets that accept the block sizes they choose.

The project is still active, though the forking strategy they are using is still not very well articulated. In fact, due to security flaws, they have been hit with a 70% nodes crash due to memory leaks.

Bitcoin Classic – Feb 2016

Still dabbling with the problem of block limits, bitcoin classic hard forked in Feb 2016. The network proposed a 2 MB.

They received some backing from major crypto users, but the block size limit of 2MB proved not popular, and they had to resort to user-defined block sizes.

The project is still running, secured by about 100 nodes, and they have a five-year plan.

They don't have an existing coin yet, and most exchanges like Bittrex are selling futures for the coin.

Introducing SegWit

As can be seen, block size has been the foremost target of the previous hard forks.

But What if there is another solution? Dr. Wuille invented SegWit.

A transaction has several components, including the digital signature that authorizes the transaction. This signature is a about 60% of the transaction size. By using extended blocks, Dr. Wuille demonstrated that the signature could be removed from within the block and stored in an extended block, the segregated witness. He made his presentation in the Hong Kong Bitcoin Scaling conference show.

According to him, this would free up space in each mined block to accommodate more transactions.

Segwit is a soft fork that was introduced under BIP 141 but implemented as a BIP 9 soft fork on 24th August 2017.

As you may expect, most miners will not be happy if the block is made to confirm more transactions. This is because the incentive to hike fees in an attempt to 'jump the queue' is no longer there.

This is how the SegWit controversy started.

Bitcoin Cash Hard Fork – August 2017

With the realization that SegWit was unstoppable on bitcoin core, some members executed a quick hard fork that produced Bitcoin Cash.

Its work started some time after the conclusion of the New York Agreement that happened in May 2017. BCH wallets started rejecting bitcoin blocks on August 1, 2017.

Apparently, many didn't like SegWit. In fact, the developers were so bullish about its success that they released it without lobbying for support to hard fork.

Quickly, they started attracting major players, like investor known as Roger Var. ViaBTC, a major Chinese bitcoin miner, also soon joined the fray.

Bitcoin cash has some very interesting features that make it have a good survival rate;

- It is supported by all the other previous hard forks
- Bitcoin miners can mine bitcoin cash and vice versa, allowing for opportunistic mining. This in effect allows BCH to enjoy bitcoin's massive hash power sometimes.
- It has a huge market capitalization, currently sitting fourth behind Bitcoin, Ripple, and Ethereum.
- It seems to benefit from bitcoin's crashes, and its price has steadily been growing.

- Its block size is 8MB which solves most of bitcoins transaction fees and speeds problems.

What is the Bitcoin Gold Hard Fork?

This is an interesting fork that deviates from the issue of block sizes.

BTG eliminates the use of complicated computers called ASICs and returns us to the age of GPUs for mining.

This has been achieved by changing the Proof of Work algorithm from bitcoin's SHA256 to a new one known as Equihash.

This algorithm adjusts the difficulty of mining with every block. This then allows for the currency to bring the difficulty back to GPU territory, which is good for many people who could not keep pace with the rise in mining difficulty associated with bitcoin.

The SegWit2x hard fork

By now it is clear that distributed consensus is not easy to handle or maintain, especially when talking about scalability, block sizes, wait times, mining difficulty, and transaction fees. These things mean different things to different members of a Blockchain.

Segwit2X was a hard fork that was heavily lobbied for in the bitcoin network, and it was designed to accommodate those who wanted bigger blocks and those who favored SegWit. With Segwit2X, block size was to be increased to 2MB in addition to the SegWit implementation that was initiated on August 25, 2017.

SegWit2x has had a tough journey with miners withdrawing their hash power agreement to mine the SegWit2X hard fork.

For it to succeed, it needed 95% hash power support, but that has not happened so far.

5.3. The Rise of the Altcoins

Emerging as alternatives to bitcoin, all other cryptocurrencies will always be known as altcoins. By the time of writing this, altcoins controlled 67% of the market capitalization of cryptocurrencies, with bitcoin taking 33%.

The market capitalization is a measure of the value of all mined bitcoins. In January 2018, it stands at a whopping $750 billion.

So what are these altcoins? Why are they emerging and becoming so popular?

Often, altcoins are created to cater for a deficiency that is perceived to be resident in bitcoin, and lately in the major altcoins that are there in the market. And these features are many and varied;

- As already seen with the bitcoin hard forks, many altcoins try to address the block size issue which has a direct implication on transaction fees and wait times.

- Others feel that bitcoin and most altcoins are not anonymous enough, allowing government and other unwanted snooping.

- Others feel that even without any scalability issues, the processing of transactions in bitcoin is naturally slow and strive to improve on that.

- There are some that have brought novel ideas into Blockchain technology, like Ethereum which allowed the world to understand that not only money can exist as a digital asset. That we could one day run whole countries on the Blockchain using digital assets and smart contracts.

- Still, in fact, Ethereum charted the way forward to enable the use of digital assets as fuels to run a Blockchain that does other things other than transfer money. This allows the resident altcoin, like ether, to be used as the fees for the transfer of other digital assets, a concept that is crucial for the survival of the altcoin as it now can allow even other altcoins to run applications on the Blockchain.

We will dedicate a chapter for Ethereum next so that the differences can be well understood. We will then look at groups of other cryptocurrencies by the functionalities they offer as an alternative to bitcoin.

6. Ethereum, The Ultimate Altcoin

When you learn about bitcoin and its ground-breaking technologies, it is sometimes hard to imagine a better way to present the Blockchain technology to the world.

But the second most important crypto in the world's ranking by popularity, even though lately overtaken by Ripple in market capitalization, is Ethereum. It adopts a massive improvement of the Blockchain technology as an alternative to most of the traditional industries, and in addition to functionalities offered by bitcoin.

What makes the Ethereum Blockchain Unique?

Ethereum is the world of Smart Contracts and the world of decentralized applications and organizations.

But first, let us go on a heritage treasure hunt in the short history of Ethereum.

6.1. Vitalik Buterin and the History of Ethereum

As Bitcoin was gaining ground as a breakthrough in digital cash transfer at around 2011, one of the people who saw the technology and quickly fell in love with the innovation was Vitalik Buterin.

A 17-year-old Canadian who was born in Russia, He was a mathematical genius and a university student blogger who was introduced to the technology by his father.

Mihai Elisie, 23, had noticed Buterin's writing on crypto blogs. Mihai asked Buterin to join him in starting Bitcoin Magazine. Buterin promptly accepted. He then became its chief technical writer.

The magazine would bring to him the much-needed exposure about the inner workings of the Blockchain technology, including the administration and improvement of the bitcoin Blockchain.

He soon identified his innovations that could be used as a massive improvement to bitcoin. In 2013, he contacted and started working with Dr. Gavin Wood to develop with him the Ethereum protocol. He quickly dropped out of college to work for the Ethereum foundation on a full-time basis, and he introduced the platform in January 2014.

With it, Buterin and his team changed the Blockchain technology as the world knew it ... forever.

The emergence of Smart Contracts

Smart contracts are simple applications. They are executable cryptographic codes that are deployed to a Blockchain where the wait to execute through a specific activity. They are programmed to be inviolable and execute exactly as programmed.

They can then be processed by the miners or validators into blocks and immutably kept in the Blockchain.

Whenever activated, smart contracts execut the code, creating other transactions that can also be stored immutably into the Blockchain.

For smart contracts to function, they have to be Touring-Complete and must be loaded with enough fuel or gas. This fuel is the payment, in Ether, that is required to compensate nodes that run the smart contract.

The fuel is critical because it allows the Ethereum Blockchain to avoid loop attacks that could be used against smart contracts. These attacks are only possible if the person deploying them is not surcharged a fuel. They could clog up the nodes and shut the network down by executing endlessly.

When working in a harmonious group to deliver more complex outcomes, smart contracts are referred to as Decentralized applications.

6.2. The Decentralized Network

All Blockchains use decentralized consensus and guarantee immutability of transactions. The Ethereum Blockchain is not an exception. The community is diverse, with diverging interests.

The Ethereum Community

The Ethereum Community is very dynamic. It consists of individuals and organizations, working together and running nodes that develop and maintain the network. These entities collectively help in the realization of the Ethereum overall goals. They include;

- **Core developers**: Led by Buterin, the developers created the original cryptographic code and continued to improve the Blockchain as intended by the network.

- **The miners**; run the nodes that confirm transactions. They also update the distributed ledger and in doing so, secure the platform.

- **Independent Developers:** Ethereum allows other people to deploy smart contracts and applications onto its Blockchain. They are a very pivotal addition to the Ethereum Blockchain as a deviation from Bitcoin's goal. With these developers, we can now dream of decentralized social media, search engines, marketing organizations, other digitization of assets and even management of public affairs.

- **Researchers** who are the technical thinkers, think and research on the key concepts that drive the Blockchain.

Once agreed that they are on the verge of a good innovation, they then let the developers and other users in on the suggestions.

- **Clients**: These are the wallet holders, and users of applications who use the Blockchain on a day to day basis
- **Organizations**: They work on the platform by funding and using applications.

6.3. Ethereum Trading Options

Speculative Holding

As stated, ether is a fuel that runs the Ethereum Blockchain. However, it is also tradable on the major exchanges as users buy it to act as a fuel to run their applications, or simply want to exit to fiat currency by buying it and exchanging it for fiat.

Though all cryptocurrency holdings are risky, Eth is one of the most flexible cryptocurrencies one can have, and it shares most trading platforms with Bitcoin.

You can hold Eth for long-term speculation if you study and believe in its increased demand and finite circulation over time.

Proof of Stake Options

We have already learned how wasteful bitcoin mining can be.

Ethereum has introduced the Dagger-Hashimoto algorithm to democratize and further decentralize of mining. This will even be improved by removing mining altogether by introducing the Proof of Stake concept for block creation and confirmation of transactions as a replacement to Proof of Work and Mining.

The PoS concept allows anyone who is operating in the network to set up a master node.

You do this by locking up an amount of ether into the Blockchain to be allowed to become a validator. Buterin suggests an initial master node lock up of somewhere around 1000 Eth per node. This figure will decrease with time to 10 Eth.

The community will then create a consensus rule on the way of assigning the block creation to those who hold the master nodes.

This way, generation of ether will be cheaper, users will participate more in the creation of the blocks and Ether, there will be increased decentralization of the network, and it will be possible to build penalties into the code for punishing master nodes that misuse their power to defraud or attack the network.

Also, with locked up Ether, it can be expected that the value of Eth will rise due to demand.

How to Judge When it is Right to Buy or Sell

There is no standard that guides one of when to buy or sell cryptocurrencies. When you invest, study ether as you would, any commodity.

Ask and get answered to pertinent questions about the asset.

- What are the features that make it unique to a coin of the future?
- How are the other competitors fairing? Who is supporting which alternative?
- How is the Blockchain marketing its popular features?
- What problems is the Ethereum Blockchain solving?

Always try to get the best options there is.

Once we present the Ethereum Blockchain in totality, you will understand how different it is from any other Blockchain, and then from there, you can decide what to do if you are joining the crypto world.

6.4. Ethereum's Unique Features

The Age of the dApps

Decentralized applications are being placed on the market to change how the world is run, and it is happening mainly because Ethereum has popularized them.

There are three types of dApps.

Money based applications which allow us to trade in money, and transfer it from wallet to wallet, peer to peer, at a minimal cost as compared to more traditional money transfer platforms. This is simply similar to what bitcoin does.

Applications that involve money and allow for the transfer of other types of data, including records, deeds. licenses, certificates, etc.in addition to the transfer of money

Other applications that do not necessarily involve the transfer of money but whose use can give absolute provenance and security of other types of transactions are also possible, for example, government systems like voting, opinion polls, and surveys.

To succeed, dApps must also be open source, reward contributors, and be operated on a distributed network

Crowd Sourced Prediction Markets

Prediction markets like betting are presented in an open source application like <u>Augur</u>. Inside them, anyone can start a betting market by funding it and inviting people to try and win a prediction.

Governments

Prevention of vices like state capture, vote rigging, and corruption can be enabled using the technology.

Land registries; The Swedish government leads in the technology that allows a Blockchain to immutably manage land registration.

Bequeathed real estate could be inalterably executed according to the distributed will of the original owner.

The DAO

When an entire organization is formed and run through cryptographic code using a combination of smart contracts and decentralized applications, and with very minimal human intervention, it can be referred to as a DAO. Buterin Posits that a DAO can be run without human managerial interference so long as it is built on a Turing-complete platform like the EVM.

After it is coded in, a coin is launched, and investors buy it with Ether. They can then use the coin to vote and can eventually earn a percentage of the profit commensurate with their coin holding.

DAOs have been proposed to run for various purposes, including as charity organizations, venture capital organizations and medical insurance firms. The most famous DAO was *The DAO*, an Ethereum based enterprise that was crowdfunded to the tune of $150 million and designed to receive proposals, evaluate them, fund them and run them for profit.

The DAO was immediately attacked and Eth to the tune of $50million spirited off, after hackers exploited flaws in the code and orchestrated a fallout about how to recover the funds.

Eventually, the Ethereum Blockchain had to hard fork. Community members who did not want to compromise the ground rules of Blockchain technology, essentially the immutability of transactions, continued mining in the old version, and Ethereum Classic was born.

The majority of the network followed the hard fork chain, arguing that common human decency must prevail over strict adherence to Blockchain rules in some cases, like when someone deliberately exploited weaknesses in the code to harm other users by draining their earnings.

If the DAO were still operational, it probably would still be setting the pace in this revolutionary technology, but other efforts that are being established now have the benefit of hindsight provided by the hack that killed it.

Ethereum's Journey; The Self-Inflicted hard forks

Many Blockchains suffer from lack of distributed foresight. If the original developers of a Blockchain do not emphasize on must-haves that protect the network especially when it finally gets the attention of the masses, issues with conflicting interests like what is currently being witnessed with bitcoin crop up;

- If there were small blocks to start with, miners refuse to vote for an increase because the queues of transactions are lucrative for them and people want to pay high fees to jump the queue.

- Governments want to utilize pseudo-anonymity etc., to access transaction data
- Hackers use cryptographic rules to attack weaknesses and hit innocent exchanges and clients etc.

Buterin exhibited a very integrated and stupendous approach to future scalability by hard-coding compulsory milestones that would see Ethereum scale the heights of these challenges to become a truly worldwide virtual reality that would appeal to the masses.

To mature the Blockchain into a world-class platform for smart contracts and decentralized applications, Ethereum divided its development into four stages, or hard forks, namely *Frontier*, *Homestead*, *Metropolis* and finally *Serenity*.

Frontier is the minimalistic version that launched the Ethereum network. It allowed for uploading contracts, mining, and the availing of ether to exchanges for trading. Decentralized applications could also be uploaded for testing.

Homestead has been a beta version of the platform, but it is where the network was declared by its users to be stable and safe. In this stage, some of the major projects are being built and operated.

Metropolis was designed to be achieved in two stages, mainly *Byzantium* and *Constantinople*. It will see Ethereum reach the street-level user interface milestone. It will be known as Mist, and it will have its dApp store. Metropolis is supposed to reveal the real power of the Ethereum platform. It will be released in two stages;

Byzantium was designed to allow the developers to boost transaction anonymity. This increases investor confidence and reduces regulation possibilities from centralized establishments.

This would be achieved by introducing a highly technical verification method used by ZCash, in which nodes do not require the actual transactional information to prove the validity of the transactions. It is called Zk-Snarks, or Zero Knowledge Proof. Byzantium was begun in late September 2017, just before the beginning of the Ethereum Ice age.

Constantinople; This will be a fine-tuning of Byzantine and an introduction of a test case for Proof of Stake. It will be the transition to Serenity, with the escalation of the difficulty bomb as the main mover to enhance rapid upgrades towards a complete switch to PoS.

The POW Timebomb

Ethereum hard-coded a difficulty time bomb into its algorithm, which is a deliberate movement from proof of work to proof of stake.

It is to be incorporated into these forks through a transitionally period where Ethereum would be created using both mining and staking.

The Blockchain will then initiate the onset of the Ice age by increasing the difficulty of mining from 15 seconds at current, exponentially upwards to a point where it is no longer economical to mine.

And that will assist in hard forking, hopefully without major community fall-outs, to the final stage.

Serenity

The final thrust in **Serenity** will be the move from PoW to PoS, achieved through the Casper algorithm.

With Vlad Zamfir, a Blockchain economist at the helm, Ethereum has developed Casper. The algorithm will be assisted by other improvements in the network by other developers to make the system faster, cheaper, easier to use for street-level people and more efficient.

The EVM – a Worldwide Computational Network

The test-net of the Ethereum protocol is an ingenious computational innovation that opens up an affordable environment for application and smart contract testing in runtime mode without affecting the stable Blockchain. It is called the Ethereum Virtual Machine

Every node that joins the Blockchain also gets the EVM, which is a completely segregated network on its own.

The EVM is Turing Complete, meaning that it can execute any code that the developers come with, and it has the time and memory provided free by the network.

Ethereum's Coin Supply

The availability of the Ethereum coin is not yet decided may rise to even 100 million before the adoption of PoS using the Casper algorithm, and upwards after that.

This is because the Blockchain developers want to encourage usability rather than storing value.

Also, the effect of capping cannot be determined from the outset due to the dynamic nature of the Blockchain's scalability. There are also the issues of unexpected developments that could increase demand for the Blockchain's functionalities.

6.5.   The future of Ether

If there will be a story of the ages to define how determined the decentralized systems developers are in bringing true decentralization using Blockchain technology to the masses, that story will include Ethereum, and its founder, Vitalik Buterin, in it.

As much as there is an undefined supply of Ether, the Casper algorithm will tie significant amounts of Eth in dormant wallets for long periods as proof of stake, ensuring that the inflationary nature of the coin's availability is stemmed and value is not dependent on the total supply, but rather on the circulating supply.

7. Other Cryptocurrencies Based on Types

As mentioned earlier, cryptocurrencies that are worth mention at current are mainly offering an improvement of one bitcoin feature or another. This chapter will have a brief look at some of these types of cryptocurrencies.

7.1. Improving on anonymity

Privacy is not the same as anonymity. Private transactions are those transactions where the particulars of the transactions are kept away from unintended prying eyes. This does not mean that the records of the transactions cannot be accessed.

It means that those who are privy to the transaction are trusted, and the owner of the transactions is confident that no other people will access the information without his say so.

Anonymity, on the other hand, is a situation where there are no trusted entities, and even though the transactions themselves can be seen by everyone, no one knows who is transacting except the person doing the transaction.

Why anonymity is important to cryptocurrency users

It is an open secret that governments detest cryptocurrencies. It is hard to pry when money is moving anonymously. It is also a certain way of laundering money and hiding crime loot.

When you control money, you have power, and you control people. Cryptocurrencies threaten the old world order and the monopolistic control that governments enjoy over their economies.

For example, the Chinese government has shut down Initial Coin offerings (ICOs) and shutting down exchanges soon. But interestingly, this is not because they don't want to use cryptocurrencies per se. There is a possibility that they are working to boost a hegemonic control of cryptocurrency use in the territories by imposing one complete Blockchain state using such cryptocurrencies as NEO, which is more or less the Chinese version of Ethereum.

With anonymous transactions, it becomes hard for the government to clamp down on the use of other cryptocurrencies.

Other governments have not been left behind in this too, as has been seen with financial institutions and regulators trooping to courts to seek for explanations of exactly how legal cryptocurrencies are.

And this is the point. People have seen a way of bypassing this control, which sometimes can go overboard, and that is why the Blockchain is as attractive as it is to them.

The anonymity technologies

There are several anonymity technologies that all try to conceal the identities of those carrying out crypto transactions.

I2P, or Invincible Internet Project, is an anonymizing software that works as a network within a network, hence keeping internet activity and identities private. Projects hidden within it cannot be found using normal search engines like Google or Duckduckgo.

TOR is a USP portable distributed anonymity kit that you can use without downloading, and it masks your activity on the internet. Even the sites you access will not be able to know your physical or personal details when you are using TOR.

zk-SNARKs, or Zero-Knowledge Succinct Non-Interactive Argument of Knowledge, is an encrypted data validation system that allows one to prove the validity of data without revealing the data itself.

Transaction Mixing uses the coin mixer technology where transactions are banged around different wallets to severe the connection between the wallet sending the crypto and the one receiving. While bitcoin's Zerocash protocol uses third parties, to do this, there is a proposal to create an Ethereum compatible decentralized coin mixing technology.

The Anonymous Transaction Cryptocurrencies

Surprisingly, both Ethereum and Bitcoin are working to join the anonymity party quite late, and rightly so. Bitcoin exchanges have been prevailed upon to provide information to governments, especially in the UK.

Bitcoin itself is a decentralized entity and cannot be asked by anyone to do anything, except its members.

They employ the technologies we have mentioned here, and they include Dash, Zcash, Mo-nero, Bytecoin, Verge, and PIVX.

7.2. Improving on Transaction Speed

Another sticky point is bitcoin's speeds, which are limited to a mere seven transactions per second. Several top altcoins have capitalized on that to create a name for themselves.

Ripple, for example, has achieved transaction speed parity with Visa, at 10,000 transactions per second by using its resident XRP Payment Channel.

Steem is a surprising second in this speed race, weighing in at a maximum of 1,000 transactions per second through the use of the Graphene technology, but with the ability to hit 10,000 transactions per second when the Blockchain gains wide acceptance.

Other notable currencies in this space are NEM (3000 tps), Monero (up to 1,000 tps), Litecoin (58 tps with a possible increase when the lightning network is adopted) and Dash (28 tps) and finally Ethereum (25 tps) and Ethereum Classic (14 tps).

7.3. The Proof of Stake Group

To do away with the traditional mining, proof of stake tries to give the block creation right to those who hold more coins in the network.

While this may be seen by some as a case of the haves vs. the have-nots, it is a credible improvement to the mining algorithm that has threatened to bring back centralization of the Blockchain through hash power distribution.

Ethereum may have started as a mining platform, but as seen earlier, they had planned to create a grand march through the mining 'ice age' to embrace Casper, a culmination of various efforts to embrace Proof of Stake.

Dash

Built on Bitcoin Core but with improvements in speeds and anonymity, Dash is one of the pioneer altcoins that employed the use of the Proof of Stake algorithm. Hodlers of Dash will, however, need to stake 1000 Dash for an annual profit of approximately 7.5%, plus the benefit of the appreciation of the hodled Dash.

With a current price of an excess of $1200 for a unit of Dash, that is a daunting investment that could pay good passive dividends.

NEO

NEO, formerly known as Antshares, has a relationship with another coin in its Blockchain known as GAS, formerly Antcoins. You can stake Antcoins on the Blockchain and earn the right to create blocks.

PIVX

Touted as the first Dash Hard Fork currency, PIVX is a coin whose acronym stands for Private Instant Verified Transaction. It boasts improved speed and anonymity, and you can open a master node with 10,000 PIVX as the stake for a 4.8% annual profit and the resultant appreciation of the price of the coin.

7.4. The Advent of Decentralized Social Responsibility

Another interesting crop of cryptocurrencies is those that seem to be entering the uncharted waters of social responsibility. And in this space, only PURA comes into sharp focus as a major upcoming player.

PURA is fronting itself as the first ever cryptocurrency that is pioneering the decentralization of social responsibility and environmental management.

The cryptographic algorithms in PURA borrow from the open-source DASH protocol but adds very interesting features that are expected to appeal to many in the society.

8. Getting Started with Cryptocurrency Trading

8.1. Introduction to Wallets

When you think of your physical fiat currency wallet, you think of storing paper money, business cards, some mugshots of loved ones and other interesting valuables.

Fiat currency is government regulated money like dollars, pounds, etc.

I have heard of tissue paper and some quite unmentionable 'accessories' in wallets!

But:

- Crypto wallets are only similar to fiat wallets in that they store money. From there, things start to get interesting;

- Crypto wallets are software applications. They are digital, just like the coins they hold.

- They can be online, or offline. When offline, we call them cold wallets.

- Cold wallets could include desktop wallets, hardware wallets or paper wallets.

- Hot wallets exist online, and some are usually held on exchanges to facilitate trading.

- Wallets must be able to support the cryptocurrencies that you intend to hold. For example, some wallets can only store bitcoin.

- You can interchange cryptocurrencies inside some online wallets.

- They have public keys and private keys. Public keys are what other people see, the identity to which they send you crypto.

Private keys are your digital signatures. They should never be shared with anyone or forgotten because they cannot be recovered, and they are the only security in your portfolio.

Wallet Choices

The choice of what wallet to have will mainly depend on the reason for buying your bitcoin. You could be intending to use bitcoin for many purposes that will dictate what kind of wallet you want to have.

- If you just want to send some money to someone in crypto, you can simply go to a peer to peer exchange, open a hot wallet, buy bitcoin, and send it to someone's wallet from the same exchange without the need to transfer the bitcoin to a cooler wallet.

- If you intend to hold bitcoin longer, for speculative purposes, it is more advisable to hold it on either a desktop wallet, a hardware wallet or a paper wallet.

- If you want to go shopping, especially if you live in a place where bitcoin is acceptable as a currency, you can hold your bitcoins in a mobile wallet.

8.2. Buying Cryptocurrencies

Once you have your chosen wallet, you can then proceed to purchase your crypto as per your preferences.

Buying from stock exchanges

While the most immediate and secure way of starting and growing your portfolio is to buy, the market has its fair share of fraudsters who operate as brokers and exchange agencies of cryptocurrencies.

But let us look at the best-established exchange platforms from across the world. (See Table 8.2.1)

Country	Platform
The United States	itBit, Gemini, Coinbase, Bittrex and Poloniex
The United Kingdom	Bittylicious, Coincorner, Coinfloor
China	OkCoin, Uhobi
Japan	BitFlyer, BTCBox, Coincheck
India	Coinsecure, Unocoin, Zebpay
South Korea	Coinone, Korbit, Bithumb

Table 8.2.1. More of this can be found on https://bitcoin.org/en/exchanges

Let us have a look at several of the international exchange platforms and how they operate;

Localbitcoins

Also founded in June 2012, LocalBitcoins has headquarters in Helsinki, Finland. Essentially, it is a marketplace which operates an escrow based protection program to ensure that money is not lost when it is transferred for buying or selling currencies.

People post their intent to sell or buy the coin, and for how much of the resident fiat currency. Those who want to do business with any posted intent will agree to pay cash for cryptocurrencies, or through online transfer.

LocalBitcoin has had its fair share of frustrations with the legal mechanisms of different countries, but its trader base continues to grow.

The site has a dispute resolution mechanism to mitigate conflicts between buyers and sellers.

Coinbase

Founded in June 2012 and with headquarters in San Francisco, California, Coinbase runs an exchange which accepts fiat currency for bitcoin, Litecoin, and Ethereum, and also trading between cryptocurrencies.

It accepts the legal tender from 32 countries and has a bitcoin wallet that is operable in 190 countries across the globe.

Coinbase exchanges can be effected through a bank transfer. When on the platform, you can trade either as a 'taker' where you pledge a fee of 0.25% or as a maker, where you offer no fee.

Bitsquare

Bit Square operates a desktop application that allows you to trade your fiat currency to bitcoin and bypass many challenges that you may encounter with other exchanges.

The site promises a simple installation and operation that can be done within 10 minutes.

Kraken

Operating mainly in Canada, Europe, Japan and the United States, Kraken is touted as one of the most transparent and secure bitcoin exchanges in the market. They are currently overseeing the Mt. Gox scam bitcoin claims.

It has the biggest EUR to cryptocurrency trading volume in the world at current. They also accept the Canadian dollar and the GBP, with no minimum deposit set to trade.

They offer bitcoin and Ethereum trading among other cryptocurrencies and are pioneers in cryptographic platform audit standards. They also have a 'maker' and 'taker' system where they charge different fees.

BitStamp

Bitstamp claims to offer cold storage for 98% of the portfolio put on their platform, which is a great step towards to assuring the safety of funds especially after they were hacked in 2015.

With offices in Luxembourg, New York, and London, they claim to be the first fully licensed cryptocurrency operator in Europe.

Their platform accepts fiat deposits directly for exchange into cryptocurrencies via bank transfer but does not do instant payments like PayPal or MasterCard.

Bittrex

Bittrex is one of the newest exchanges, and they are prominent on security and speed. Built in the US, they promise fast and easy deposits and withdrawals while guaranteeing the unrivaled quality of service and security.

All trading fees are set at a flat rate of 0.25%.

Purchase on exchanges (exchanges/stock exchanges (review of reliable), five most popular and the principle of purchases).

Poloniex

With over 80 coins on its platform, Poloniex is one of the biggest and most diverse crypto exchanges in the world. It has a double verification account opening system for security purposes.

Based in San Francisco, US, the exchange was established in January 2014 by Trista D'Agosta, and does not accept fiat currency. However, it has a very smart trading screen and a very transparent fee structure based on the taker/maker model. The makers have a higher fee, and lenders are charged a flat 15% on interest.

Also, due to the volume of trading on the platform, it tends to be slow, and their support can be quite frustrating.

Bithumb

This is a little-known cryptocurrency exchange that is generating very intense Bitcoin Cash, Ethereum and Litecoin Bitcoin to fiat exchange traffic. Other coins on offer at this exchange include the Dash, Litecoin, Ripple, ETC, and Monero. It is only providing a Korean Won fiat exchange, which understandable if the traffic they already have is anything to go by.

Based in South Korea. It is the largest cryptocurrency exchange in a country that oscillates between third and fifth in digital asset trading in the world.

Curiously, though, it doesn't support a BTC/ETH trading pair. Bithumb has developed bitcoin gift vouchers, with the smallest fiat value being around 10,000 Kow. It also accepts them back for a change into an equivalent bitcoin value.

Curiously, it is the world's biggest exchange for Bitcoin Cash, Litecoin, Ethereum, Ripple, and Dash, Displaying a very interesting trend in altcoin interest in the East.

Bitfinex

If you want to trade as a corporate, Bitfinex is the place to go. This is because it allows margin trading, has very good trading rates and boasts of a huge lender market. It has among the largest amount of crypto traffic in the world. Founded in 2012 by Raphael Nicolle and based in Hong Kong, the exchange has a primary focus on crypto traffic from the US.

Their security features seem to be top-notch, but like anything else on the net, they have lost millions of dollars to hackers, especially during the August 2016 heist in which 120,000 Bitcoins worth around $72million at the time were lost.

However, they immediately issue their token (BFX) to affected customers as security and have since managed to buy back all the BFX for BTC, which has made them among the most trusted exchanges in existence.

8.3. Tips When Trading in Cryptocurrencies

If you want to make money with cryptocurrency trading, you must always have a few pointers on how to go about it to make sure you do not lose money.

Trade only when you have a reason

"Of course I have a reason to trade – to make money!" you might say.

But you must also realize that you could lose money if you do not watch out.

For example, if you decide to enter a trade for a coin because of an impending hard fork, you must be optimistic that the hard fork is widely accepted and will create a media buzz which will attract other buyers.

Trading crypto is a zero-sum game, meaning that your gain is someone else's loss. It is led by whales who pump prices up by buying an altcoin for a time, and then dumping it to small people like you and I when we come calling and collecting profits from our loss.

Spotting the Scams

Ponzi and pyramid schemes litter crypto world like landmines in a world war II battle zone. They mask themselves as mining pools, membership forums or even ICOs. You need to learn how to study the white papers behind any of the smaller altcoins.

Who are the development team behind the coin? Who supports the ICO? How reachable is the supporting team? Which known entity endorses the token? These are questions that you must run in your mind and look for answers before plunging.

Choose your trading route

To trade any currency, you need to research on several things to make your trade smooth and hassle-free.

- How will you buy the coin? You need to check whether you can buy the coin using other cryptos like bitcoin, or through fiat, which exchanges you will use, etc.

- How will you store the coin? You will need to have a hardware, desktop or mobile wallet where you can secure your portfolio during the trading periods.

Establishing your target and Stop loss options

Cryptocurrencies can gain and also drop in value in minutes.

If you are certain that a rise is imminent for a crypto you are holding, say by 100%, set your trade target at that level and collect your gains while you are still ahead.

Crypto is unregulated and highly volatile, so don't stretch your luck.

Conversely, you should also set your stop loss to a level that you are comfortable with to bail from a losing trade before you lose all your hard-earned coins. This will allow you to make a hard decision to cut your losses, but at least you get to live to fight another day with what you salvage.

Spread your risk

As in everything in life, diversification is a good risk management strategy in how you hold your crypto portfolio.

What coin are you holding vs. what is happening to its network?

What is your distribution of crypto holding? Are there some coins that are in your portfolio and have not been traded for some time?

Whatever you do, watch every dime. Give yourself time to understand every coin you hold, its dynamics, etc.

Understand Bitcoin's role in the trades of other cryptos

Altcoins are valued in comparison to Bitcoin.

If bitcoin is going through a volatile period, then it may not be wise to trade in crypto for the moment.

If bitcoin is gaining, altcoins have a decline in their bitcoin value. You, therefore, need to set very close targets, be mean with your stop loss options or simply not trade at all.

Buying into crowd-sales

One of the most exciting ways of making a kill is buying tokens during crowd sales.

This is because the tokens are usually offered at a low price, and if the idea of the crowd sale is of importance to the world, the coin will start trading on main exchanges and therefore will rise in value.

However, it is important to fully grasp the idea behind the token, the team working around it, the ease of selling your loot when you need to bail, etc.

Trading Options

Several options exist for trading crypto-currencies. While some people simply buy crypto-currencies and hold, it also possible to buy into fu-tures, or use leverage trading on platforms like eToro and Plus500.

Day trading is a good past time with people who know how to work with various altcoins and can switch currencies quickly. Ideally, you need to have good internet, an impeccable understanding of exist-ing markets and a willingness to keep your finger on the button to buy or sell as you do your research.

You can also invest some money into pool mining, but as this book has variously pointed out, most cryptocurrencies are getting away from specialized mining in favor of Proof of Stake and other consensus algorithms.

Another way of investing in cryptocurrency is through creating your cryptocurrency, especially if you have a killer idea that can be upscaled through crowd sales.

9. The Future Value of Bitcoin and the Altcoins

There are over 1000 crypto coins in circulation. The Blockchain technology can no longer be ignored. A wealth of over $750 billion is held by bitcoin and the altcoins.

Some people will gain a lot of wealth and others will lose, depending on the intrinsic value of the cryptocurrencies they hold. The failure of most coins will be mainly because they of fraud especially when they have no value and are just created to prey on the gullibility of the people who invest in them.

Other coins will make those who invest in them millions of dollars from practically nothing. If Laszlo Hanyecz had not used his 10,000 bitcoin in 2009 to pizzas, he would now be worth a staggering amount of money.

The other good thing about cryptocurrencies is that most of them are simply keys to a Blockchain that performs far more important functions than the coin itself. In other words, to most of the modern day Blockchains, the coin is an incidental mode of trans-fer of value. This guarantees the coin life and an ever-increasing value because its users will continue to value the Blockchain and therefore use the coin.

10. Governments and Cryptos: Prohibit or Lead

Governments are as dumbfounded as the cryptocurrency developers have been with the ever increasing uptake of the Blockchain technology. It seems people were yearning to gain financial privacy and the power to do as they wished with their money. However, some cases are unique. Governments have rushed to regulate how bitcoin is handled and how information is availed for scrutiny, and yet there exist several examples of friendly co-existence of bitcoin, the altcoins, and fiat currency.

10.1. Japan

When Coincheck announced that it had been licensed to operate as a legitimate 'virtual currency exchange' in Japan on September 13, 2017, the cryptocurrency fraternity heaved a huge sigh of relief. One of the biggest world economies had just endorsed the Blockchain technology after it had received huge publicity body blows from China and the US in the preceding days.

Japan accorded recognition to Bitcoin on April 1, 2017, as a form of payment. The government did this to protect Japanese users of cryptocurrencies and to formalize usage.

10.2. The US

America could be making concerted efforts to ensure that entities do not hide money in crypto assets, and as a result, have created the inadvertent effect of educating even more users of the power of cryptocurrencies.

When the IRS asked Coinbase to release the crypto wallet information for all unknown users for the years 2013-15, the signal was out. The government was waking up and smelling the cryptic coffee. When a critical mass of a country's economy threatens to move from the traditional markets to the Blockchain, regulators have to look for ways of regulating.

And while this may be disappointing to a few people who wanted to stay longer in the anonymity provided by the Blockchain and rake in untaxed profits, it is important for cryptocurrencies to be recognized by governments so that the path to mainstream acceptance becomes easier.

10.3. South Korea

South Korea has among the most intense cryptocurrency activity in the world. It is the fifth in the world. The Central Bank there has sensationally admitted that "cryptocurrencies and fiat currency coexist." Also, the government there is busy looking for ways of regulating cryptocurrencies.

10.4. Austria

There is a cautious approach to the adoption of cryptocurrencies by the Austrian central bank. The Governor, Mr. Ewald Nowotny, has moved from comparing the cryptocurrencies to the 'Tulip Craze' of Holland of the 16th Century, to saying that the country cannot ban them as they would a banknote.

It is now possible to exchange Euros for bitcoins from any post office in Austria.

10.5. Spain

With a declaration that bitcoin is essentially money that does not have VAT exemption, Spain has set the pace for the adoption of cryptocurrencies as a widely accepted means of exchange in Europe.

Recently, the major banks like Banc Sabadell, EVO Banc, Abanka and Banco Popular in Spain made a deal with BTCPoint to avail over 10,000 ATMs for bitcoin to cash transactions.

Thus, with 0% commission charged on transacttions, BTCPoint has entered into direct competition with Bet2Me, another exchange that charges 1% commission in the same market.

10.6. China

While China recognizes the need to take the lead in the development of Blockchain technology as one of the developing economies of the world, it has recently found it necessary to rein in the advent of crowdfunding.

They have affected this clampdown with a freeze of all exchange activity on their main crypto exchanges. When BTCChina announced that they would be closing down all exchange activity from September 30, 2017, due to this, the bitcoin and all the major currencies received a massive drop in prices within days.

However, the Chinese government has been reported to be working with NEO to create the first ever Smart government.

11. Resources

11.1. Blogs:

- On Famous Quotes:
  https://medium.com/@MartinRosulek/1
  4-bitcoin-quotes-by-famous-people-
  6e7a1a009281
- Blockchain of the future:
  https://www.shapingtomorrow.com/ho
  me/alert/665529-Future-of--Blockchain

11.2. Exchanges:

- https://bitcoin.org/en/exchanges

11.3. Detecting Pumps and Dumps:

- https://medium.com/@vyacheslave8ni/c
  rypto-currency-trading-pump-and-
  dumps-noobs-guide-3a3c71f21522

11.4. Wallets:

- To buy www.cryptowallets.org/
- Free wallets: https://freewallet.org/

11.5. For White Papers

- http://startupmanagement.org/2014/12/16/the-ultimate-list-of-bitcoin-and-Blockchain-white-papers/

12. Conclusion

We have tried to put a lot of the concepts that go into a primary understanding of what bitcoin and the cryptocurrencies are, why they have caused such a big splash in the financial industry, and why the future looks bright for the cryptocurrencies.

We have tried to put a heavy representation about the literature around bitcoin because, without a proper understanding of what bitcoin is, there cannot be a true conversation of what other crypto-currencies promise.

After going through this text, it should be possible for you, the reader, to make your first steps in cryptocurrency trading.

From deciding what cryptocurrency, you want to hold, you can choose the platforms that trade it, how to install the wallet that will hold it, and for what purpose you will be buying the currency.

We have also tried to infuse a good sense of heritage and history on this unfolding technology to prepare you for the truly interesting times that we will surely face ahead.

Hopefully, you have received what we promised you during the introduction, and that you had an interesting read!